Navigating Without a Compass

*Tools to Survive the Challenges of
an Adopted Child with Special Needs*

Dana Estlund & Sharon Broome

Navigating Without a Compass:
Tools to Survive the Challenges of an Adopted Child with Special Needs

Copyright © 2019 by Dana Estlund

ISBN: 978-1-7342317-0-0

Published by Hope Publishing Partners

Edited by Patricia Cox

Cover design by Nanjar Tri Mukti

Book layout by Robert Louis Henry of RightHandPublishing.com

Contact the authors at withoutacompass1@gmail.com

Dedications

From Dana

First and foremost, I would like to dedicate this book to my best friend and mentor, my mom. Thank you for everything you have done for me! You have been my rock throughout this whole journey as well as my life, and I could not have handled this challenge without you. You are the "Wind Beneath My Wings" (Bette Midler). We make a good team!

To "our village" including all the psychiatrists, therapists, doctors, teachers, and school personnel who have made this journey a little easier by being there when needed and believing that this child would not have had a fair chance in life without all of the support of the village.

To Beverly for keeping me on track while helping me to understand a behaviorally-challenged child. Thank you for supporting me through this difficult journey with many ups and downs and validating that my thoughts and feelings were normal.

To Meg'n for helping me through the struggles of taking on a child with special needs and for all of the creative out-of-the-box ideas.

To my closest friends for listening to my rantings, helping me through my tears, and giving me support throughout the years. I could not have done it without all of you.

From Sharon

First, I want to thank my husband Joe for your patience during the long hours we spent writing our book, for your steadfastness during times of crisis, and for your ability to listen and give us good advice.

To all my dear friends, who listened unconditionally, gave great advice, and offered loving support to Dana and me.

To my parents for their gift of humor that has allowed us to see the lighter side of life.

And finally, to Dana, who dared to undertake the adoption of a son with special needs and refused to give up, through difficult circumstances, so that he could have a "forever home." It takes a special mother to love a child who cannot easily reciprocate love and exhibits anger without provocation. I love and admire your strength.

Contents

Prologue

"It is usually the deepest pain
which empowers you to grow to your highest self." – Unknown

"Not again," I thought with disbelief! Tyler, my adopted 17-year-old son with special needs had been doing well for a couple of months. He had been able to control his anger fairly well recently. Sure, he had the same issues as other teenagers – moody and self-righteous, insisting that I'm always wrong, but also fun, joking, and somewhat normal at times. In the past few weeks, his episodes of stealing, sneaking around, moodiness, and manipulation had increased. I thought this was just a temporary increase in his behavior that would level out again. Then I found out he had stolen coins from his father's collection on a weekend visitation and transferred them in his cheek to our home and eventually to school. While he was grounded for that incident, I discovered an overwhelming odor of propellant in his playroom, which he vehemently denied for days. I finally discovered the truth that he had taken the propellant from the garage, hidden it in his sweat pants, transferred it to his playroom to "shine" his collection of cars, and threw it out his window to avoid being caught. Of course the room

1

reeked! I was totally blindsided and furious! I was trying to give him more autonomy, including short periods of time without direct supervision. I felt totally betrayed - again!

His consequence for this misconduct was being grounded in his room. His anger reached a dangerous level, but instead of taking it out on himself, as he often did, he planned an escape. On this cold day in November, after getting the screen off his window, he jumped 20 feet from his second-floor bedroom to the ground, with no coat or shoes and headed off with only a blanket wrapped around him. What had happened to this relatively decent kid and what was I going to do? I couldn't believe I'd been deceived again. How many more times could I go through this roller coaster of emotions? I've tried so hard to be a good parent. I thought I had the answers. I'm writing a book that has no end – at least not one with a predictable outcome.

My purpose for writing this book is to share my story about adopting and parenting a difficult child with special needs. By sharing my struggles and successes, I hope that my readers will be able to relate to common issues and themes that we may have with our children and to be able to use some of the tools that I have found useful.

When I began my journey, I had no idea what would lie ahead of me but knew I had fallen into a deep rabbit hole very early in the process. It has been the single most difficult thing I've had to do in my life. Despite all of the early chaos, my path has improved over time. It may not be perfect or what I thought was perfect, but tolerable. I have survived. And you can too!

Each child is a unique creation with innate characteristics. These, combined with environmental and situational circumstances, interact to create the individual. Each family unit is different in its makeup and dynamics, and each child with special needs carries with them a set of diagnoses and behaviors that define their personality. We were novices trying to find our way through a disorganized system, with no guidebook or compass to follow. This is true for most new parents without the added challenge of special needs. The foster care system fails novice parents, and there are huge challenges to overcome.

What I learned was gained through trial and error, intuition, word of mouth, and a desperate search for resources. Trust your feelings, your own intuition, and judgment. You know your child better than anyone else. What worked and didn't work with Tyler may be entirely different than what you're experiencing. Different kids have different issues. I have learned that I have to continually advocate for him every step of the way and in every situation, such as with his school, his therapists, and the healthcare and mental health systems. Hopefully, you can find ideas and information in this book that will help make your journey easier. For this book, I have changed my son's name to "Tyler" to protect his privacy. At the end of the chapters, I have included my mom's perspective throughout our journey.

Chapter 1
In the Beginning

My dream was to have a child someday and I had thought about it for years. However, "life happened" and I found myself nearing 40 without having that dream come true. So I approached my husband about it. He said he still wanted his own child, and did not want to consider adoption yet. So we tried on our own to get pregnant. I went off the birth control pill and was pregnant within less than six months. However, it ended in a miscarriage. By this time, I had turned 40 years old and decided I didn't want to have a natural birth due to complications that could occur giving birth at a later age. After discussing the idea with my husband again, I felt that he agreed that our best option was to adopt. We didn't want to go out of the country for a child since we knew there were many unwanted children right here in our own state ready to be fostered and adopted. So, we started exploring our options.

After numerous calls, I found there was a website that listed all the available foster children. I researched online for each county in our state where available children were listed. I saw several young children that seemed interesting but when I called the county to inquire about them, they said the website was very outdated and they were at least three years older at that time. This was the first issue we encountered with the broken foster care system. After exploring further, I learned that the process to become foster parents was lengthy and included a six week class and a home-study, where a caseworker interviews the spouses separately, and then together. We also had to be fingerprinted. Once everything was completed and approved, we were cleared for fostering children and assigned a caseworker.

> ***TIP:*** *Adoption assistance subsidies are available from the Department of Health and Human Services' Division of Child Welfare for foster-to-adopt families who adopt children with special needs. This stipend is to assist with additional costs of hard-to-adopt children and can often become an on-going monthly stipend after adoption. You might have to do some advocating for this stipend on an ongoing basis due to your child's higher needs. (Child Welfare Information Gateway, 2011)*

After approval as foster care parents, we decided we wanted an infant since we knew bonding would be a huge issue. Our caseworker kept us informed of potential matches, and we were called a couple of times. Infants are hard to adopt because a family member often takes the child before they are available to the public. This happened to us twice. We were still in the search mode for the right fit. I happened to get an email from

The Adoption Exchange of Colorado, stating there would be a get-together with foster families and their children for placement in foster-to-adopt homes. It was at an amusement park in Denver. We attended and thumbed through their book with pictures of all of the children at the event. While we were looking for a young child, we happened to see a picture and information for the youngest child there at age five. He would someday become our son!

> *TIP: Some lessons learned: The first is that the "system" does not give specific classes on each of the diagnoses of the child. That is detrimental since parents like us have no idea how those diagnoses affect the child's behaviors. If the child has a medical or psychological diagnosis, do your homework and get more information before bringing the child into your home. We have learned a vast amount about our son's diagnoses, after the fact, through our own research. The second lesson is to make sure you and your spouse/significant other are both on the same page and engaged in the adoption process. I was unaware until right after the adoption took place that my husband did not want to adopt a child. He never gave me any indication that he was having second thoughts until it was too late. This issue presented many problems down the road. The third lesson is adopting a child with special needs is a lifetime commitment. Some are never able to live independently and may need supervision all their lives.*

I know there are many couples who decide children are not for them and that is fine. When we were married at 28 and 30 respectively, we each said we wanted a maximum of two children. We were successful in our lives and were enjoying our fulfilling careers and each other's company. Everyone, including ourselves, perceived us as having a good marriage. Time just started getting away from us. I've always loved kids and had done a lot of babysitting and working in a daycare center, so being a mother was a natural desire. My husband was the youngest of three children, and he had no parenting experience. But we had built our relationship into something we thought was very strong. At the time, I thought things were so stable in our lives that I was a little bored. I wanted a change of some sort, believing bringing a child into our lives might be fulfilling.

I was very excited to increase our family but had no realistic idea of what it would entail. We thought a child would only change our lives 50%, but it was actually 100%. My friends still laugh with me about it and ask me if I feel the same way now. This experience changed not only the way we lived but the way we communicated as a couple. Even though we were on the same page with parenting ideas most of the time, it put an enormous strain on our marriage. I didn't want to be part of the high statistic of parents that divorced after a foster child came into their lives. Unfortunately, our divorce still happened, ten years later when Tyler was 15.

We were first introduced to Tyler at the amusement park event enjoying the day with his foster parents and their son. The boys were on the riverboats and had just gotten off of the ride. They were laughing and playing around. They looked like they were having a great time. Tyler had a little bomber jacket on and was so cute in it! We met his caseworker, who introduced us to the foster parents and the boys. Tyler was the little one with freckles, blue eyes, and a mouthful of silver fillings. That was the first thing I noticed when he smiled. The boys left to continue enjoying the park. We thought he was great and made it clear that we were interested in him.

Over the next few weeks, I frequently contacted his caseworker. Having to follow up continuously was a reoccurring theme throughout our journey, whether it was with the foster care system, teachers, therapists, doctors, or specialists. I can't say it enough – ADVOCATE, ADVOCATE, ADVOCATE – for your child whenever and wherever you can. I called Tyler's caseworker and emailed him at least once a week. We found out later that one of the main reasons we were the chosen family, out of several interested in him, was that I was so persistent.

When his caseworker called to say they were considering us as his foster-to-adopt parents, we were thrilled. Words couldn't describe how excited we were to be potentially starting a new chapter in our lives with a new five-year-old addition to our family. We met with the caseworker to give us all of the documentation informing us about his past. Overall, it was minimal information, and there were many gaps to fill in. We found out that his history included domestic violence, physical abuse, sexual abuse, drug exposure, and neglect. His biological mother used crack-cocaine for the first six months of her pregnancy. Therefore, Tyler's brain did not develop normally during pregnancy, and he now has below average intellectual scores. Not only does he have Intellectual Disability Disorder (I/DD) but he also has many behavioral issues from being a foster care child in the state system from age three to five. We were his sixth foster home. Our caseworker used a great analogy, which helped to explain his situation. He said to imagine attaching a piece of duct tape to a sweater. This bond represents the initial parent/child relationship. If you then take the duct tape off, it will now have sweater residue on it. If you try to attach it to another sweater (or another home), the tape sticks less due to the accumulated sweater residue. By the time you do that six times (or six homes later), the tape (bond) is very minimal, or not at all in our case.

The documentation also stated that Tyler was ranked a "5" out of "5" on a risk scale, but they said they would be reducing him to a level "4". We thought that was a good thing, but had no basis for understanding the rankings. Apparently, the score was lowered because the foster parents said he had not been doing any of the bad behaviors he had when he had come to them (peeing in corners, smearing feces on walls, harming animals). We had no idea what all of it meant and accepted what the case manager was saying. We thought this was a good sign and that our future foster son seemed to be improving. Later, after Tyler came to live with us, we saw similar behaviors reappear and realized they hadn't improved, but were just dormant for a while. He was still a "5" in dysfunction from our perspective.

After contemplating the decision over the weekend, we told his caseworker we would gladly accept him into our home as his "forever family." We were very green and new to all of this. It just seemed exciting! We realized later that telling our child he's moving to his "forever home" left no perceived option of returning him before the adoption, in case the trial period wasn't successful. In my opinion, it is detrimental to the child and the foster parents to promise a "forever home" until the adoption takes place.

> ***TIP:*** *If your caseworker tells you they are looking for adoptive parents with no other children in the home so you can concentrate on raising this child, TAKE THEM SERIOUSLY! I think it's their "code" for "please take this child off our hands." Of course, these children are probably most in need of a loving home, but get all of the facts before making your final decision.*

We were preparing for him to become a part of our family, so we decked out his room with a small television, bookshelf, and computer. We understood that he liked Spiderman and Thomas the Train, so we decorated his room that way. We found out later he actually didn't like them, but everyone thought he did because he imitated others around him. We were told that he needed to be in a home with no other children so he could try to "find" himself. It was quite some time before we figured out what that meant. We discovered later that he was still very naïve. He had little self-awareness. He was unable to tell us his favorite color or name favorite foods. He had no idea about traditions such as Christmas, Santa Claus, the Easter Bunny, or birthday celebrations. Except for his previous foster home, it seems that he was ignored for most of the first five years of his life.

The transition from Tyler's foster parents to our home happened pretty quickly. We had a one-on-one meeting at their home and enjoyed dinner together. He was watching us and seemed to be sizing us up in his mind. The meeting seemed to go well. The next time we met with him and his foster parents was at a car show. We took him on our own for a bit without them, walked around, and ate some ice cream. Things seemed to go well. The next step was taking him to an air show without his foster parents.

This last outing was the first time we had a chance to talk with him alone and began seeing a bit of his dysfunction, although we didn't understand it at all then. He called us "Mom" and "Dad" on that first encounter. We thought that was odd since he also called his foster parents Mom and Dad. After only one day that we'd been with him, he transferred those labels to us, not knowing who we were. He was also calling his grandma "Mom", not understanding roles within families. We found out later that this is a typical problem with Reactive Attachment Disorder (RAD) kids because they've never bonded with their biological mother.

In June of 2007, he moved into our house. This day was the beginning of a *long* and *hard* journey, down a path that we had no idea would evolve the way it did!

As grandparents, we were excited that our adult children wanted to start a family and that they had chosen to adopt a child. We followed their progress from our home in Florida, and we were thrilled to see pictures of prospective children in the foster care system. We knew that there would be challenges of adopting a child but, like Dana and her husband, never thought to do any research on how it might affect them or our families. Her husband's family had concerns that he had never expressed an interest in having children before, and perhaps Dana did push the issue more than she should have; however, we felt they were adults who could make their own decisions. We were happy that they were branching out of their comfort level to experience parenthood. My generation never gave "choice" a thought as to whether to have children. We just had them! It wasn't always such a good thing either.

Chapter 2

Is This What
I Signed Up For?

The day had finally arrived. We were excited to start this next chapter in our lives with a new addition to our family. We had already gotten his room ready and put a big "Welcome Home" banner on the garage. He was wide-eyed and curious when we drove up. We thought we could tell what he was thinking and what promise he saw ahead of him in this new life. I realize now that he was totally unaware. After all, he had done this five times before. It was a pretty good first twelve hours, and then things rapidly went downhill. We didn't realize how much of a bumpy ride this was really going to be. What had we gotten ourselves into?

The first week, and specifically the first 24 hours, was probably the most challenging time I had ever dealt with up to that point in my life. Before having him come live with us, I was elated at the thought of having a child. I had been looking forward to this event for so many years.

However, reality hit quickly, and depression set in. I was devastated. We were grieving about what we had just done. We found out later that this is quite normal, whether it is an adopted child or a biological child. I was experiencing something like Post-Partum Depression, which, for adoptive parents, is called Post-Adoption Depression Syndrome (PADS). (Child Welfare Information Gateway, 2015) We were doubtful. Did we do the right thing by bringing a five-year-old child with significant behavioral problems into our home?

It seemed as though it was an unwritten rule that we were all supposed to get along and love each other from the moment he stepped into our home. A close family member told us, "You should be in seventh heaven right now after adopting a child. What is wrong with you? All you need to do is hug him and love him, and everything will be fine." Wait…hold on a minute. Even family members were not supportive of how we were feeling? What is wrong with this picture? What just happened? What was wrong with us? I honestly thought there was something wrong with me for not being so happy about all of it. I kept asking myself these questions over and over again, but the depression and anxiety were so overwhelming that I couldn't even think logically. That first week I could barely get out of bed each day. I was feeling a huge loss of self and a massive loss of freedom with this significant life change - much more so than I would have ever imagined.

At that time, I only had questions and no answers, which brought me no comfort in this daunting process. Did we make the right decision? Did we have the option of giving him back?

Would we want to make that choice of putting him back in the foster care system? What would it do to his psyche after we had told him we were his "forever family"? I felt guilty that I was even having these thoughts. Eventually, we found out that many people go through the very same thing, questioning everything. We realized we weren't crazy or horrible people. We had taken on something incredibly complex, but didn't know how difficult. Eventually, it got better, but it's important to feel what you feel and not feel guilty about it. Humor has probably been the most effective tool that has gotten me through the tough times, with a lot of tears in between.

With depression and guilt setting in, we realized quickly that we needed help in dealing with our situation, and we needed it immediately. We discovered that it was very typical to feel overwhelmed, exhibiting symptoms of severe fatigue and stress, and often having an increase in illnesses. As a matter of fact, I was sick eleven times in the first year! We felt very guilty that we couldn't say we loved him, or even liked him at the time, due to his behaviors. This was the beginning of the "village" of support people we needed for our own mental health. Our village has continued to grow over the years and includes family, friends, therapists, psychiatrists, doctors, teachers, school administrators, tutors, community programs, special needs funding sources, and respite programs.

Foster parents and potential adoptive parents often hesitate to talk about their feelings to anyone, thinking it might jeopardize the adoption. We have trouble even admitting these thoughts and feelings to ourselves. But during those early tumultuous times, we realized we needed help and couldn't do it alone. We tried to keep the professionals informed of what we were going through. We received enormous support from them, even though they didn't have many concrete ideas at the beginning either. It felt as though he was "attached to my hip" at all times, and I just wanted to "shake him off". I was feeling so helpless. I have found out since that time that he is very complicated with many diagnoses contributing to his behaviors. Older children who have been in many different foster homes, like Tyler, often have multiple psychological issues and problems with trust and attachment. His known diagnoses at the time of fostering him were sketchy, and minimal, but included Attention-Deficit Hyperactivity Disorder (ADHD), Post Traumatic Stress Disorder (PTSD), and possible Reactive Attachment Disorder (RAD), along with exhibiting symptoms of other possible diagnoses.

I've listed some of his behaviors. Perhaps you have experienced these with your own child.

1) Using bodily fluids in inappropriate ways: urinating on the carpet in front of our bedroom door, in his bedroom heating vent, or on the school bathroom floor, and spitting/drooling at random

2) Spreading bloody boogers on the wall

3) Hoarding hundreds of NutraSweet packets in his room under furniture, in drawers, and the closet

4) Having severe tantrums (melt-downs) at home and school (head-banging, throwing things, stomping feet, slamming doors, screaming, inappropriate noises, whining, high-pitched sounds, dragging himself along, pouting, and self-harming behaviors, such as scratching arms/legs with water bottle caps, plastic items, hitting himself to make bruises, choking himself)

5) Exhibiting an affinity to fires (attempting to light them using various objects, sticking objects in electrical outlets or shooting water into the outlets, batteries)

6) Stealing items from school, peers, and home, and then hiding them in unusual places, such as sprinkler boxes, behind furniture, in his sleeves, in his clothing

7) Having lots of tics (shoulder jerking, picking fingers, toes, and the bottoms of his feet)

8) Eating lots of weird things like paper, food off the floor of the movie theater, and the insides of desiccant packets you find in pill bottles. When we took him to a movie for the first time and I was immersed in the film, I looked over at him and noticed he had a mouthful of a paper napkin. I guess we needed to feed him more!

During the first weeks of Tyler joining our family, our lives felt miserable. Before the adoption took place, it would have been helpful to have had our county human services provide classes focused on his diagnoses. We had to discover on our own that he had no concept of cause and effect, no remorse, insight, or conscience, and had sensory, trust, and safety issues. He hoarded, stole, and then hid his stash. These deficits, coupled with the previously described behaviors, made us realize this was not going to be easy!

Due to his tantrums, we eventually had to remove furniture in his bedroom, piece-by-piece, until finally just leaving a mattress and bedding on the floor. Over time, he destroyed the dresser drawers, his closet doors, his TV and computer, and pulled all the decals off his walls. He ruined a bedside lamp with little fish "swimming" on the rotating shade by pouring water onto it. We laughed to ourselves when we took friends on a tour of the house and they saw numerical keypads on some of the doors and his bedroom stripped down to a mattress. It looked a little like a jail. We always gave them an explanation about his uncontrollable tantrums, which probably gave them something to talk about on their drive home. But these measures we put in place kept him safer and us saner! This was a very complicated child that we had brought into our home.

A few months after his arrival, we planned a trip with our new foster-to-adopt child and our friends, which became a very pivotal event. We had no idea how to deal with a child with so many challenges and should never have gone anywhere so soon. A normal child might have adapted to the trip more easily than Tyler. The trip involved getting up very early each day and staying up late. Meal times were irregular and we weren't getting enough sleep. We thought he would fit into our flexible life, without realizing that at the time he needed a routine and predictable schedule. There were several adults on the trip but no children with whom to play. He was alone in a sea of people he didn't know and hadn't bonded with us either. When he acted out, we tried time-outs as discipline. The more we tried to get him to behave, the worse he became. We were able to adapt to the challenge by moving into our own hotel room, committing to afternoon rests and earlier bedtimes, and maintaining regular meal times. This was irritating to our friends because it was different than what we all normally did on our trips together.

Some of these friends thought we were being too strict and offered unsolicited opinions. We felt judged by the people closest to us. We were not getting the unconditional support we thought we should have and needed from them. I was feeling very guilty and alienated, and I lashed out at them. I was defensive and not a very nice person during this time, which probably was not at all helpful. But, I was human and dealt with it the best way I knew. After that trip I had no interest in continuing "friendships" with the people I felt had betrayed me in my greatest need for support. Over time, this incident created friction between my husband and me. He later shared that he resented my refusal to go on future trips with the group and that he missed those friends.

I often wondered if we would have gone ahead with the adoption if we had known then what we knew later. Eventually, over time, I was able to "fake it until I made it" when I felt there was no reprieve in sight. And it really did get easier over time, *Lots* of time! For me, it has been a slow progression with many setbacks – three steps forward, two back – with many

21

surprises along the way. Now, I'm glad that I was willing to take the risk and stick to the decision I made. This process has been a positive growth experience for both Tyler and me.

Dana and I have always had a great relationship. Even while I lived in Florida, we stayed in touch, talking several times a week by phone and sharing our feelings, concerns, joys, and challenges. We were, and still, are best friends. I followed the progress of their finding their child and then bringing him into their home. Soon after that, the phone calls increased to daily or even hourly, as his behavior worsened and Dana's fears and frustrations increased. I felt helpless so far away, yet I had a job that required I stay in Florida. I was unable to break away and physically help her. I felt guilty that I wasn't there to help. She had been telling me that she was depressed, but I didn't realize the depth of it until one weekend.

We were on vacation with family when I got a telephone call from her early in the morning. Dana was in her bedroom when she called, so depressed she couldn't get out of bed and face Tyler, questioning whether it was too late to send him back. Completely out of energy and resources, she didn't think she could face another day with him. The only thing stopping her was that the foster system had told him that this was his "forever home." She told me that she couldn't disappoint him.

Even in her desperation, she was still putting his needs before her own. I felt helpless but knew I had to remain strong for her at that moment. We talked a lot about where she could get some immediate respite. I'm not sure of all the steps she took that weekend to find resources, but there was only one viable alternative at that time. Tyler's former foster parents agreed to take him for the weekend. It took some pressure off for the moment and gave these exhausted parents some much-needed rest. One lesson learned from this would be for new foster parents to set up some respite alternatives ahead of time before bringing a foster-to-adopt child into your home. Another lesson was that the situation affects not only the foster parents but their family and friends. It was difficult to stay strong for her when I needed someone to hold me up too. Somehow I managed. Looking back, we all grew stronger from this experience.

Chapter 3
Adoption Day

Another six months went by, and the Adoption Day was nearing. Unfortunately, my anxiety continued. How would our lives unfold after the adoption? Would any of Tyler's behaviors improve over time? Would they get worse? Would we have to give him back at some point if they didn't improve? Once the judge declared it final, we couldn't reverse it. Could I handle this? All of these thoughts were going through my head at the time, but I pushed forward continuing to tell myself this was the best thing for this lost child. I just wasn't sure if it was still the best thing for me.

It was evident during these six months that our son did not fully understand what it meant to be adopted and continued to have negative behaviors. He was leery of believing we were his "forever family" and would only call us by our first names. I vividly remember a bath time close to the adoption date where Tyler said, "When I go to my next home…" I gently responded, "This is your only home now. You will not be moving to anyone else's house. You are stuck with us, and we are stuck with you." He grinned. I said, "Since the adoption is going to take place, it is ok if you want to call us Mom and Dad." He finally did, and when that happened, and when I honestly thought he meant it, I think it was one of the most significant bonding moments we had early on in the process. I actually had a bit of hope!

The day was finally here. We were going through with the adoption. I still was feeling an array of emotions but was relieved that it may all work out for the best, and continued to have high hopes!

In May of 2008, we dressed up in our best clothes and headed off for the next chapter in our lives. We arrived at the courthouse and met some of our friends, family, Tyler's caseworker, and his therapist. I'm not sure he understood everything, but he seemed to be happy during the event.

We walked into the courtroom, flanked by everyone, and sat down. The adoption proceedings started, and much of it was a blur to me. One thing that stood out in my mind was the Guardian Ad Litem (GAL), his attorney advocate, kept saying over and over again, "These people are saints." In his mind, we were the perfect family and the ideal fit for this child. I sure didn't feel like a saint but had hoped it would get better over time. At one point during the ceremony, the judge requested our presence at the podium. With a grin, the judge told Tyler it was ok not to eat his Brussel sprouts for at least a week, since this was such a special day for him. Tyler thought this was a great idea, and he still remembers it to this day.

We left the courtroom and spent the rest of the day visiting with friends. We ended the day at Red Robin Restaurant and told them that we just adopted our son, and were celebrating. They were very excited to hear that. We ordered our food and waited and waited. Finally, the whole staff showed up with a cake from the grocery store next door, several gifts for him and said the dinner was complimentary. What special people they were and what a wonderful memory we had of our Adoption Day. Having a support system and the village in place (even strangers) is *huge* in this process. We needed this happy memory to begin to look more positively toward our long future together.

Chapter 4

First-Year Post-Adoption/Finding Respite

After the adoption took place, we encountered new hurdles. We found that as soon as the adoption was over, all support was cut off from our county's human services. Tyler's therapist was no longer able to see him. His caseworkers had cut off communications, and his GAL, the advocate who was supposed to be watching out for him, was nowhere to be found. It was a huge eye-opener and a significant detriment in the long run. All support had virtually stopped. This network and village we had created in the mental health system for almost a year was gone, non-existent. The boat had left, and we were now in the water floundering. What were we going to do? What resources did we need to keep us afloat? We found out the hard way about advocating for our son and ourselves and have continued to do so throughout the years.

My husband and I had recent significant changes in our employment situations. I decreased from full-time work to part-time upon our son coming to live with us. My husband's job changed to where he was traveling much of the time, leaving me with virtually no support, while raising a child with behavior challenges. I felt so alone in all of this, and it put a considerable strain on our marriage.

I needed to find Tyler another therapist since the one he had was discontinued by social services. Because of my added stress, I procrastinated searching, which turned out to be a big mistake. I tried not to blame myself because I knew that I did what I could do at the time.

About seven months post-adoption, our child's teacher noticed him having increased difficulties in school. He was already on ADHD medication, which had been prescribed by a physician in his previous foster home. He seemed to be responding well to the drug, so we continued with it. At that time, one of his doctors thought he might be eligible for more anti-anxiety medication, so he referred us to a psychiatrist. We met with her for a 45-minute session without Tyler. She asked a series of questions and determined *without seeing him* that he might benefit from Zoloft, an anti-anxiety drug, and prescribed it. She said we should see positive results in about two weeks.

> *TIP: Children should never be prescribed medication without being seen by the physician first. I should have intervened, but I didn't know better at the time. The more you know your child and the system, the more you can trust your judgment and question health care providers.*

After about six days, we started noticing major changes in his behavior. He became very agitated, aggressive, mean-spirited, and angry. His actions escalated to a new height, which included self-harming. We had no idea how to deal with him. Tyler ended up having a full-blown, major tantrum in his bedroom, where he destroyed everything and piled the remains in the middle of his room. He also sat at the table with food dripping out of his mouth and laughing hysterically. We panicked! We had never seen these behaviors to this extent before and were exasperated trying to control him so he would not destroy the house, himself, or us. During this tantrum, I wrapped my arms around him, and snuggly held him to try to calm him down. Nothing we did worked, but this worn-out child finally fell asleep about midnight, from sheer exhaustion. I was in tears and felt helpless for both him and us. What were we to do at this point? I know the psychiatrist said we would see some changed behaviors. I thought they were supposed to be positive. Why weren't they? Would he get better over time? Should we "ride it out" and see what might happen? Who could help us now?

We decided to let Tyler sleep in the next morning and go to school a bit later. He woke up and seemed to be in a little better mood, so we took him to school. Not long after, I got a call from the principal saying that he was destroying things, throwing pencils and rocks at the teachers, and being very defiant towards everyone. I was in tears and asked the principal what we should do. He thought the best thing would be to take him to a children's hospital for evaluation, which we did.

> **TIP:** *Make sure you thoroughly evaluate the credentials and references for all medical health personnel (physicians, therapists, and psychiatrists) to ensure you are getting the best care available for your child. We made a big mistake the first time by not doing so. Since then, we have searched and found the best mental health professionals out there. It has taken much time and effort to make sure we have the right care in place. I am now very cautious about changing or adding new medications without careful research and a slow transition process.*

Our introduction to the Colorado mental health system did not go smoothly. Getting emergency mental health care was new to us, and the system appeared extremely fractionated. We spent the next five hours in the emergency room, repeating our story numerous times to the different staff members. The consensus was to admit him to a mental health unit for evaluation. Unfortunately, there were no beds available at this hospital, so they took him by ambulance to another mental health facility with available beds. We have learned that there is a tremendous nationwide shortage of available mental health in-patient beds for children and teens. We were so naive at the time and new to children's mental health and hospital services that we had no idea what to expect.

> **TIP:** *Make sure you do your research ahead of time and be aware of what hospitals and settings would be best if a crisis arises with your child.*

We arrived at the new location at about 11:00 p.m., so all the patients were asleep. As we arrived, we noticed how drab and dreary the hospital appeared. It had an unpleasant odor and left a bad first impression. We were all tired and emotionally drained at this point. They took him into a holding area for the night since he was still not assigned to a room. I know Tyler did not understand the scope of what was happening, nor did we. We were under the impression we would be staying with him. That was not the case. As they got him settled in, they took us out of the room and said we could go home and get some sleep. I was devastated.

Since the building was old, the walls weren't very sound-proof. As we left the facility, I could hear our son screaming and wailing, "Where are my mommy and daddy?" Though sad, we felt a glimmer of hope that he had bonded to us, evidenced by his crying out our names. He needed us, after all! We had been telling him that we were his "forever family," and we would never leave him. What we were doing was contrary to what we had promised. I was weeping as we walked out and collapsed in the parking lot. My husband had to help me walk to the car. I was utterly devastated. As I sit here, writing this, it is bringing up all those raw memories again, and the tears have started flowing. It was probably one of the lowest points of my life.

Tyler was in the hospital for at least a month while they tried to regulate his behaviors and medications. We had no idea it would take so long. We visited him twice a day for weeks. The hospital was about an hour's drive from our house. This difficult experience was all-consuming. We found out the medication prescribed for him, Zoloft, had triggered his bipolar/depressive side; therefore, it allowed him to release all his pent-up anger. The doctors were continually adjusting his medications to regulate his emotions. Each time a new drug or a new dosage was changed, it would take three to four days to see if it worked. Consequently, the hospital stay was extended more than we anticipated; they told us this was quite normal in many cases.

During our child's stay, he was able to come home with us for a couple of overnight visits. He exhibited new behaviors we hadn't seen before: hitting himself with rocks on his forehead and banging his head on the sliding glass door. He was still angry. We were unsure how this was all going to unfold. We, again, questioned whether we had made the right choice by taking on this responsibility. Even though it was agonizing, I kept reminding myself, "Yes, we are still doing the right thing." I was determined not to send this child back. Our home was going to be his "forever home" because we had promised him, the system, and ourselves.

I recall an incident that occurred during one of our hospital visits to see Tyler. He said he needed to go to the bathroom. When he came back, there was something all over his shirt. I asked what it was, and he said, "It is taco meat from lunch." I smelled it, and it was feces. Yuck! He had taken his feces from the toilet and spread it all over his shirt. This behavior is typical of abused children, and my son had previously been known to smear feces on walls. I didn't make a big deal of it and told him to change his shirt. I let the staff know about the incident.

There were some valuable lessons we learned during his time in the mental hospital. First, Tyler needs to be on medication to stay stable. He was previously on medication for ADHD but wasn't on any psychiatric medications. The doctors tried several drugs during his hospital stay and found that Seroquel, an anti-psychotic medication, was the best for mood stabilization for him.

Second, the hospital used a "red, yellow, green" stoplight concept for teaching him acceptable behavior levels. If he received a green light from the staff, he was doing a good job and rewarded. When he received yellow, he was warned not to go further with his actions. When he had a red, he would receive a consequence for his actions. This concept was one of the few he understood at the time; we continued to use this system for many years afterward. He didn't like it and pushed the limits continuously, but at least he understood where he stood with his behavior. For us, it was a godsend!

When Tyler reached his teens, he needed in-patient services again for suicidal thoughts and anger. This time he was fortunate to be admitted to Children's Hospital mental health unit. We saw such a difference in the quality of care he received this time. We fully support the need and funding for expanding mental health beds specifically for children.

Dana and I talked by phone throughout the incident. After they got the call from the principal, Dana called me as they drove towards the school, not knowing what they might encounter. I felt so helpless, but apparently, he was calmer when they picked him up and made their way to the emergency room. After hours of not hearing from her, I was relieved when she finally called to tell me what happened. Leaving him at the mental health hospital was very traumatic for all of them. I felt helpless. It was during this incident, and the days that followed, that I decided to retire so that I had more flexibility to help them and provide respite. It took another year before I could leave my position and have the time to give them some relief. Then, my husband and I were able to spend three to six months in Colorado every summer for about five years until we moved there permanently. So much of the time, Dana and her husband were left on their own to manage this difficult child. I felt a lot of guilt during those years that we couldn't be of more help, but now I realize that it was good for them to find their way, as all new parents need to do.

Finding Respite for Parents with Young Children

I'm sure most new parents feel a sudden sense of entrapment after the arrival of a child. Our new five-year-old came with an established set of behaviors and a history of unimaginable trauma which severely affected his personality. He couldn't be left alone and needed someone with him all the time to provide safety and security. We realized quickly we had no safety net, no backup help. He threw incredible bedtime tantrums, causing exhaustion, fear and anxiety for us.

Tyler's entry into our home immediately changed the relationship between my husband and me. We could no longer go out for dinner or to a movie as a couple. Our son's behavior interfered with normalcy inside and outside of our home. Because of his meltdowns and his need for consistency, we created a system of "tag-teaming" each other. This method allowed each of us to get away for a few hours on the weekends for some much-needed respite. During the week, we were both trying to work our regular schedules. My husband was able to "escape" each day to his job outside the home. I worked from home and was able to work a reduced, flexible schedule during this time of crisis. I was alone and responsible for this child during the day, in addition to trying to work. Tyler was terrified to be by himself and would not leave my side. I desperately wanted to hide from him and life, secluded in my room with the door locked. When I took a shower, he would lie at the entrance to the bathroom, waiting for me to emerge. Exhaustion and depression overwhelmed my husband and me. We definitely needed relief from this precarious situation.

Because Mom lived so far away and had a full-time job, we established frequent, sometimes hourly, communication by phone. She was able to provide support and ideas that helped during the immediate transition. I began searching for local support groups or persons with whom I could talk. I contacted our adoption outreach worker, support groups, and began seeing a mental health counselor. Life became somewhat more manageable.

> **TIP:** *Finding respite for parents with children with problematic special needs is all-consuming. Start by assessing your child's unique limitations – physical, psychosocial, and safety. Consider the number of hours of help needed, caretaker qualifications required and whether you will seek in-home or center-based care. The cost of care is a considerable barrier, and financial resources will be discussed later in Chapter 13. Explore the availability of respite grants from your county's Community Centered Board (Colorado Department of Health Care Policy & Financing, 2019). Friends and family members may be uncomfortable offering physical support with your child's care. Instead, ask them to help you make phone calls and do internet research to help find resources for you.*

I knew that I needed someone who was available to talk, to listen, and to be an unbiased friend and support when I was at my wit's end. For me, Mom was that person in most cases; however, there were times when I felt she was judging me and wasn't on my side. Thank goodness we were able to work through the issues and grew closer as a result. I think it's healthy to have a confidant to tell you things that you may not want to hear, to act as a sounding board, and to give you fresh ideas. Many times, there is not just one right answer, and it helps to discuss it further to figure out the best course of action. Sometimes we tried a solution and realized it didn't work after all. Finding someone you can laugh with about those trying times is one of the best stress-relievers that I found. Hopefully, you can identify someone special for yourself. It may be a spouse, family member, a counselor, a spiritual resource, or a good friend.

Other Suggestions for Respite with Young Children

- Equip the child's room with a door chime to hear when the door is opened. You can place chimes on windows for additional safety. I've listed more ideas in Ch. 10 – Safety.

- Suggest swapping childcare with another family who also has a child with special needs.

- Use drop-in daycare, by the hour – expensive but worth it!

- Teach a friend or family member how to care for your child. Sometimes they feel better if they pair up two at a time until they develop a comfort level with your child.

- Hire tutors in place of parents' dealing with homework.

- Search the internet for adoption support groups and local organizations to help provide you with information and unconditional support. See examples in the Bibliography.

- Explore extracurricular activities for your child such as classes in swimming, art, music, karate, dance, and yoga. There are free recreation center activities and after-school sports (Unified Sports or Special Olympics). After-school sports gave me time to take a breather and decompress. It also was a way to meet parents of other children with special needs.

- Nap or rest alone every day.

- Take a bubble bath/shower to help relax you.

- Sitters and Nanny Services (such as Care.com and SitterCity.com) were marginally helpful for me. My experience was they can be unreliable, costly, and time-consuming if you are seeking a good sitter/nanny who fits with your child. The ones who could drive Tyler to activities worked the best for me.

- Grandparents could take him for a day or overnight.

- Friends could volunteer to take him to a movie or after school/weekend activities.

- During our divorce settlement, my husband and I agreed to take him on alternate weekends, allowing me to have much-needed downtime every other weekend.

Dana was right when she related that she didn't always feel supported by me, although we maintained a great relationship throughout. I heard all of these problems from a distance so I couldn't directly observe the situations she described. I didn't want to doubt her, but I felt that when I was uncomfortable with something, I needed to let her know. Sometimes she was willing to hear me; sometimes, we disagreed. We learned the hard way that it was important not to approach sensitive subjects late at night or immediately after an incident happened. Patience and timing were important. We were always able to work through the situations, and we both learned how to ask and answer questions more objectively. I wanted to make sure she was doing the right thing for Tyler, and sometimes, I needed more input to feel comfortable. She wanted me to understand and to be supportive of the hard work she was putting in raising this atypical child. As grandparents, we have to tune into supporting our adult children's parenting style and

giving advice, while not overstepping the boundaries. Now that we live in Colorado, I occasionally still offer my observations and suggestions. I'm not always right, but at least I've presented my ideas. She can think them over, talk with his counselors, and present her thoughts back to me. This is what a good confidant can do to help parents of these children. Be a sounding board for them – know when to speak up and when to be quiet. And be there for them no matter what.

Chapter 5
Elementary School

During Tyler's elementary school years, his behaviors changed over time: some improved; some worsened. New ones emerged. It took two to three years after adoption before I knew he was bonded to us. One of the best things that resulted from his mental health hospital stay was that he was assigned to a new psychiatrist and therapist, both of whom were excellent clinicians and a perfect fit for our child and us.

Tyler's new therapist was as perplexed as we were about how to get through to him and to manage his odd behavior. It wasn't clear what control Tyler had, or didn't have, over his behavior. It was also unclear what he was *able* to learn versus what he was *willing* to learn. He could be quite stubborn. During this time, we were learning how to live with one another. He was figuring out how to live in his new home, and he was struggling academically. His therapist said that we would not be able to measure him academically until we got the behaviors under control. So, our primary goal during these initial years was to work on his conduct.

> ***TIP:*** *Make sure your child has an IEP (Individualized Education Plan) or a 504 plan in place in the early years of their education. This plan is extremely helpful in getting the school supports in place that your child will need to help them succeed. The Individuals with Disabilities Education Act (IDEA) is a law that requires schools to provide specialized services to children and adults with intellectual and physical disabilities (US Dept. of Education, 2004). The IEP is the plan, updated annually, that specifies what types of accommodations the school must provide to your disabled child. Parents should participate in the development of the IEP. We also invited Tyler's psychologist and others involved in his life to the IEP meetings.*

Here are some ideas that worked with our son:

- We placed chimes on both Tyler's bedroom and play-room doors. The bedroom was for sleeping and timeouts. The playroom was for fun, but a safe room. I could take a shower knowing he was in a safe space and could hear the chime if he opened the door.

- We gave immediate rewards and consequences, not cumulative; offering "carrots," or promised rewards never worked. Some examples were: If he could get his pajamas on and his teeth brushed quickly, he could play with his game for 15 minutes. If he could finish his breakfast in 10 minutes, he could watch TV until the bus came.

- As he got older, I could extend the interval between his action and his reward. An example was: If he maintained a good attitude before school in the morning, he could play his Nintendo DS after school. We were occasionally able to string a few days together for an even bigger reward, such as a special pair of shoes he wanted.

- We implemented parental reinforcement.

- We used tough love and consistency with both parents on the same page.

- We praised him immediately for good behavior as he wanted to please us.

- We created consistent routines for meals and bedtime. I think this is most essential to children with special needs.

- We used a kitchen timer to set deadlines to complete a task, such as finishing breakfast, going to the bathroom, or tasks that had become control issues. It helped to remove us as the "bad guys."

- We used computer time, computer games, and Nintendo, as rewards.

- We signed him up for Unified Sports (soccer, basketball, flag football) and encouraged physical activity such as bicycling and swimming.

- We took advantage of the before and after-school care program throughout elementary school.

Here are some ideas that worked for *all of us*:

- When Tyler had major tantrums with a lot of noise coming from his bedroom, such as thumping, screaming, and throwing things, my husband and I took turns going outside on the porch or the garage for a few minutes where we couldn't hear him. This reprieve helped us to de-escalate and regain composure. After he quieted down (sometimes after hours), we could then go into his bedroom and try to soothe him with words or a hug. Even now, when he is pouting or acting out, sending him to his room until he can turn his attitude around works well for both Tyler and me. He often can de-escalate on his own now.

Here are some ideas that *didn't* work for us but might work for you:

- Reasoning with him when he was upset

- Trying to get the truth right after he lied. It was better to wait. Later I would tell him I didn't believe him and what I thought the actual story was. Often he would give me the truth after a couple of days when I asked him again.

- Time In/Time Out – using minutes to sit quietly

- "Chicken Burrito" (swaddling in a blanket for comfort) or using a tent (his space)

- Arguing with him about body functions that we had no control over. Some examples were his chewing food without swallowing, picking his fingers and toes, spitting, drooling, and retaining his stools. Ignoring these behaviors worked best.

- Putting coins in a jar to reward good behavior. For example, after 50 pennies accumulated, he could buy something. This reward never worked because he needed immediate, not delayed, consequences.

- Stickers, as rewards

- Rewarding good behavior might work for the moment but didn't work as a deterrent for the next time.

- Meetings with police officers, again and again, as a deterrent to stealing

- Individual Sports (Tae Kwan Do, gymnastics, swimming, skateboarding). He was uncomfortable for a variety of reasons. Perhaps he was fearful of putting himself out there.

We explored different types of private and specialized schools but decided it was best to keep him in his current elementary school, since they knew how to handle him. We planned to move into a new home in another school district the summer after he completed elementary school. The school staff helped make the transition from one district to the other by facilitating a meeting. Included in the meeting were the teachers, the learning specialist from his elementary school, and the new special-needs teacher in the middle school. Initially, this was a huge help. We thought it was going to be an easier transition, but we were wrong.

Our grandson was having a terrible time in school. His problem with memory interfered with his retention of new information. In spite of lots of repetition, he would forget within moments something we thought he had just learned. He dropped farther and farther behind in school. He couldn't or wouldn't concentrate and fidgeted all the time. Having something in his hand to fidget with helped a little, but his frustration level still interfered with his tutoring. He told us he was "stupid." I came up with some games to play with him to make learning more fun. Since he seemed to respond well to the "Red Light, Yellow Light, Green Light" concept we learned from the mental hospital, I decided to use it for a game. Tyler would move forward after the right answer (green light) and backward for a wrong one (red light). We played it on the stairs using math flashcards. He loved the game but had no recollection of what the addition/subtraction flashcard answers were, even though there was a reward if he won. No amount of repetition made an impact. The more I watched him struggle, the more I realized our sweet little

grandson had a significant problem with learning. Dana and I discussed what I was observing, and after more testing, they discovered that he did have serious learning issues.

Chapter 6
Middle School

We weren't sure how well Tyler would handle the move from one school to the next one but we felt it was the best time. With a new home, new school, and new teachers, we now saw new behaviors. Thank goodness, my parents began visiting Colorado for a few months every summer to help us.

I had done a lot of preparation for the move to a new school, including meeting with his new teacher and the school staff, which I did every year. I hoped that all would go well. I emailed the principal and teacher, to remind them Tyler needed to have a modified schedule due to his "mild to moderate" disability status on his Individualized Education Plan (IEP). Children with this classification can normally function in a general classroom setting with accommodation to meet their specific needs. I emphasized he would need to have supervision before classes since he was prone to getting in trouble when left alone. I thought they had everything in place for a smooth beginning. The first day of school turned out to be a disaster!

Tyler came home from school that first day and, after lots of probing, I found out he had a regular schedule, not a "modified" one. What happened? I thought I had been clear with them and that everyone was on board. Instead, I felt I had been ignored. I sent another email to the principal and the teacher. His teacher had unintentionally dropped the ball and apologized. Classes were quickly modified, and he was on his way to starting a new adventure into middle school. We were all on this new path together without a compass to guide the way.

One issue that created lots of problems for us was that Tyler had a severe problem with memory. If the teacher told the class they were going to do a project or go on a field trip the next day, he didn't remember. He might have said to me that he had a project due but couldn't remember any of the instructions. If he finished homework that needed to be turned in, he would come home the next afternoon with it still in his backpack – sometimes for weeks. He couldn't remember to turn it in. Vital information that needed to be conveyed to me or to his teacher had to be communicated directly through email, not through my son. His forgetfulness hasn't changed much since the first day of school and is a continual source of frustration for me.

Another hurdle I encountered was that after-school daycare was no longer an option for us, unlike elementary school. In our area, once children turn 13, they are no longer allowed to attend daycare centers. I have found there is a considerable lack of resources for children between ages 13 and 18 years of age. I had to quickly start to think creatively about what resources I could use for daycare. I found Care.com and SitterCity.com online and contacted numerous caregivers to see if they would be interested in "babysitting." The main problem was there were no experienced sitters with knowledge about 13-year-olds with special needs, requiring line-of-sight care. Line-of-sight means that he needed to be physically within an adult's sight at all times.

I finally found someone willing to take care of him, who had some experience with children with special needs. She watched him after school, for school holidays, and summer vacation to do a variety of activities. But, she did not follow the guidelines that I outlined for Tyler for line-of-sight care. He was able to subtly manipulate her into doing what he wanted even though it may not have been the best for him. Daycare for a child with special needs is a significant problem for parents; we have to be creative to find solutions. Chapter 7 addresses additional respite ideas.

I felt constant stress and anxiety throughout his middle school years. We were always on guard in case negative behaviors suddenly appeared out of nowhere. And they did many times, creating constant tension in every aspect of our lives. My emotions during these tumultuous times vacillated between anger, guilt, betrayal, self-doubt, and confusion.

Nancy Thomas' book (2005), *When Love is Not Enough: A Guide to Parenting Children with Reactive Attachment Disorder* was particularly helpful to me. There are other useful books and resources in the Bibliography.

> ***TIP:*** *A word of caution - professionals sometimes disagree with techniques suggested in a book or website. Always discuss new ideas with your pediatrician or mental health professional before implementing them.*

Tyler had some classes with normal children (called neuro-typical) and other courses with children having special needs (called neuro-diverse). When he attended general classes for neuro-typical students, he had trouble keeping within his boundaries due to the lack of enough supervision. He would wander the halls, going through classrooms alone hunting computers to look up adult sites, and stealing things. I was finally able to convince the school the importance of having an adult with him at all times when he was navigating between classes, to and from bathroom breaks, and also during class. Building this requirement into his IEP has nearly eliminated episodes of his getting into trouble.

He was also having a lot of problems with homework. Tyler would come home with incomplete assignments. Since he didn't understand the material, he would instead, find other things to do to get into trouble. He was also bringing homework home that was way beyond his understanding. Something quickly needed to change. The homework would pile up. He was always many assignments behind. Helping him with homework after school was a nightmare and we had many battles over it, so we decided to use a tutor. That was a huge help that I would recommend to eliminate unnecessary arguments.

I contacted Tyler's teachers about the homework issues and told them it was ineffective for him; I insisted that he have no homework. If it didn't get done at school, it was not going to get done. I am not sure many parents are brave enough to tell the school not to give homework to their child, but I meant it! They finally got the hint and stopped sending it home. It took a lot of back and forth communication to get that accomplished. My advocacy eventually paid off.

As the year continued, his behavior got worse. He had been suspended five times during the middle school years and included both in-school and out-of-school suspensions. Nothing seemed to work, although in-school suspensions (in the principal's office) worked better than out-of- school (at home).

We knew Tyler had many diagnoses, and we suspected that he was Autistic and might also have Asperger Syndrome (a condition on the Autism spectrum). We needed to have proof for him to be provided extra resources through the school. We set up numerous meetings throughout the year with his teachers, the school psychologist, the occupational therapist, and the principal. It was getting worse, not better, while I continued to advocate for one-on-one supervision in school. They finally initiated additional testing for him and confirmed that he was indeed on the Autism Spectrum. This diagnosis was pivotal for us to get additional funding. In addition, he was now placed into the school's Significant Special Needs (SSN) program where he was able to receive higher-level services.

Toward the end of his eighth-grade year, he took his obsession with fire to a new level. He started a fire in the boys' bathroom with paper towels and a Bic lighter he found in the art room. Due to this behavior, Tyler was "in-school" suspended. He had to sit in the front office with someone at his side the entire day. He was very angry. The fire incident prompted the principal to arrange a meeting with school administrators, teachers, and the school security officer. All this time, I had been trying desperately to get everyone's attention to get more help for us, the school, and my son. Tyler told me, without question, that if he got hold of another device to start a fire, he would. He has continued to state that throughout the years - not to harm anyone intentionally but because it was "cool" and "smelled good" to him. Tyler does not understand that starting fires could be very harmful even after numerous conversations about its danger. I told the school staff that if he got another chance, I felt that he would definitely start another fire. I didn't want the school to burn down because of my son. That statement got the attention of the principal - finally!

As a result, a threat assessment was conducted by the school. The assessment included an interview with our son, where they asked questions about his feelings and possible suicidal thoughts. We were interviewed, as well as his teachers. I requested a meeting through our county human services department to get everyone on the same page about his needs. The county spokesperson said most of the time these meetings were court-mandated but agreed to participate, at my insistence. Advocating for Tyler and ourselves was imperative to assure that he got the best care possible.

There were about 15 people in attendance including Human Services staff, the school principal, teachers (both for middle school and high school), the school psychologist, Tyler's psychologist, and the Lead Behavioral Specialist for the school district. The opinion of the group was unanimous. Everyone agreed that he was a very complicated child with developmental delays, as well as atypical behavior. Most kids have either one or the other but not both. We never knew which behaviors were coming from which traumas in his past life. The group agreed that he was a good kid overall, well-meaning, and wanted to be liked. However, he was (and still is) very manipulative and sneaky, which complicated resolving the problem. He did what he was supposed to do at the moment, but couldn't transfer that information outside of that particular setting. A therapist equated his behaviors to trying to keep water in a vase with a crack in the bottom. No matter how much we want to help him learn by practicing techniques over and over again, the "water (learning) would drain out" and not stay in the vase (brain). He was not processing as a healthy brain should, probably due to his biological mother's drug use during her pregnancy.

Several conclusions were reached at the meeting. It was felt that his transition to high school might be particularly rough. His ability to transition could be the deciding factor whether he would stay in the public school system or be required to transfer into a "high-needs" school within the district. They finally agreed that he needed to be assigned to someone who could provide direct line-of-sight care at all times during his day. This requirement is still in place in high school and has been the best decision that was ever made. Unfortunately, at the meeting, the Human Services Department felt that we already had everything in place to help him and had no additional ideas, so they closed the case. I found this to be a bit unnerving since *we* were still trying to find answers and didn't feel this was enough of a plan. The system had once again failed us, and the search for more answers would continue.

My husband and I were spending time in Colorado each summer, but we weren't able to offer respite for Dana and her husband during the school year. Eventually, we moved to Colorado fulltime. We knew Tyler pretty well and had installed many safety features in our home as well (door chimes, lockboxes). We watched him while they took a trip one summer. He frequently stayed with us overnight so they could get caught up on their rest and spend quality time with each other. As Dana stated earlier, the stress of having a child with special needs takes a toll on a marriage. I was able to attend school meetings with her as support and to advocate on her side. We also visited a lot of possible private schools, potential summer camps, and private tutoring programs, such as the Sylvan Learning Center, Learning Rx, and explored some "out-of-the-box" concepts such as Brain Balance Centers,

EEG Neurofeedback, and EMDR Therapy. None of these learning techniques was a fit for him. My husband has been a big help in providing good male role modeling and quality time with him, riding bikes and providing other experiences such as car shows, sports events, and just hanging out together.

Chapter 7
Respite for
School-Age Children

Summer Vacation and School Holidays

Camps

Finding camps is a process of trial and error, specific to our children's issues, likes, and dislikes. Towards the end of spring, watch for listings of summer camps in the newspaper or online. Several of the organizations for children with special needs also post a list of camps. The local Community Centered Board provided us with a $1,000 grant for summer camps, so I tried several different ones the first summer. None of these were explicitly for kids with special needs. And, none of these worked for him, either because of his avoidance of others (Asperger's) or because he didn't receive enough supervision.

My mom and I spent a lot of time each spring searching for camps that were best for Tyler. That first year, Lego camp was interactive, but due to his tendency to avoid others, he wanted nothing to do with the other campers. At the art camp, he became bored after two sessions and refused to go again. The local recreation center day camp didn't have enough supervision. He did what he wanted to do and ate high-carbohydrate junk food for six hours straight. When I picked him up at the end of the first day, I could not get him to calm down. He was so over-stimulated. Cake camp was a complete disaster. At the end of the third day, I picked him up and noticed he had icing all over his chin, carrying a box of half-eaten cupcakes. They spent most of the time running around eating all the candy they wanted while only a couple of campers were baking in the kitchen with the instructor. The others were unsupervised in a room full of jars of candy.

There were other limiting factors. Ages and functional abilities of the children in camps were a problem. Recreation centers for "therapeutic" kids focused on the more physically and emotionally high-needs children. My son is high-functioning and physically healthy, so the planned activities in these centers underserved his needs. He was bored.

Recreation center activities or classes for non-therapeutic kids tended to overstimulate him and usually lacked adequate supervision. Often age limits of camps didn't match with his delayed maturity. Frequently, the children were much younger than him.

Other barriers were lack of available transportation and long travel times to and from camps. At age 17, I still haven't found any supervised public transportation options for him and have to drive him to camps and pick him up. Providing transportation is extremely difficult as a single parent and added hours to my very long day. Regular camps with a high ratio of camp counselors to campers (greater than 1:4) without line-of-sight supervision weren't safe. Overnight or out-of-town camps were not compatible with Tyler's needs for monitoring, heavy bedtime medications, and schedule.

> **TIP:** *I eventually found that the right types of environments for him are called "therapeutic, or adaptive" classes or camps, and I have learned to look for that term when searching.*

I found two camps in our town that worked well because both of them took children with similar diagnoses and behaviors as Tyler. One, sponsored by Easter Seals, had a variety of year-round services nationwide, including summer camps for 6 to 18-year-olds. The second camp served 16 to 21-year-olds and separated higher-functioning young adults from the more disabled. My son's group went on outings every day, so he stayed physically active and mentally stimulated, surrounded by peers with similar issues. Camps such as these have specially trained staff who have an affinity for kids with special needs and enjoy interacting with them.

Additional Ideas

- The afterschool program in elementary school was beneficial for us. The teachers all knew Tyler and how to manage him. Unfortunately, he aged out, but they were willing to take him through the summer after the

6th grade. At afterschool daycare, he would get into trouble from time-to-time. It was difficult for the staff to watch him all the time with so many other busy little kids around. They creatively taped off a large section on the floor near the front desk with duct tape. This section was "Tyler's space." He was encouraged to play in that area where they could watch him. He seemed to like "his space," and it seemed to work at least for a while.

- Bringing him into my home office to do quiet activities or watch TV while I worked was an alternative for short periods of time.

- I used his playroom as a safe space to play while I worked. Neither his playroom nor his bedroom doors were ever locked. The chimes we installed on both doors alerted us whenever he entered or exited those rooms. These chimes gave me peace of mind and a break from constant one-on-one supervision while keeping him safe.

- Look for a Boys and Girls Club in your area. Children are supervised in the clubs and must be signed in and out by a parent. They are also very affordable. Unfortunately, there were no clubs close to our home.

School breaks of any length plus summer vacations present difficulties for most parents who work. They are especially challenging for parents of children with special needs. Children who cannot be left alone complicate our options even more. Dana and I worked as a team to find Tyler suitable childcare and camps for school break times. Sometimes she would purposely select a camp that was closer to our house so that my husband and I could provide the transportation and give Dana alone time to get in her work hours. Sometimes Tyler stayed overnight with us for one or two nights to decrease her need to drive him. She explored using the bus service for the disabled, but none would pick him up from her location. Short-notice changes in schedules during the school year, such as three or four day weekends or teacher planning days creates a problem finding childcare at the last minute. Tyler often stayed home during those times doing quiet activities while Dana worked, not ideal for either of them. Somehow, we've been able to patch together a summer plan that has worked. However, we all breathe a sigh of relief when school starts each fall!

Chapter 8
Navigating the School System

Tyler came to our home just before entering his kindergarten year, which he was repeating. We felt that the upcoming year would be a difficult transition time for him – new to our home and the routine of school as well. He would be in class for a half-day and then go to the afterschool program the other half. We also explored Montessori schools and other private schools, but none could take him because he needed more supervision than they could provide. Montessori schools encourage independent self-learning, and he was definitely not independent. We ended up leaving him in the public school in our neighborhood, working within the school system to create a plan that worked best for him. This decision was a good one as I developed a great rapport with many of the teachers and administrators. He was well-liked and did learn some things along the way.

Parental Involvement

I've previously discussed the importance of parents' involvement with our children's school and to advocate for their needs. Assess your child's specific requirements so that they can be included in their Individualized Education Plan (IEP). Don't be afraid to ask for what you need. Be persistent! Initiate meetings with the teachers and daycare staff at the beginning of each school year to talk about your child's needs. At the meeting, share a list of your child's main issues, traits, and potential behaviors. (See example in Appendix) Establish an ongoing communication system between the teacher, school counselor, and yourself. We also worked out a system for times when he needed extra attention. The teacher (or another designated person) would send a daily email informing me how his day went and whether they had any concerns. I could then follow up and report back to them how the evening went and what specifically to watch for - stealing, tantrums, choking himself, or other unusual behaviors. I also suggested that the teacher keep Tyler close to their desk and slightly isolated from other children's desks. He loved helping the teachers, and this helped to decrease distractions. Having him close to the teacher helped to control his temptation to take things from the other children.

For my son, line-of-sight was a critical requirement. Because this was unusual and expensive for the school to provide, we encountered a lot of resistance. As previously mentioned, after several incidents of stealing, using unattended computers to access internet adult sites, and starting a fire in the bathroom, the school agreed to provide a fulltime teacher's assistant for him for line-of-sight.

Other effective preventative measures

- Adult-supervised walking to and from the school bus, his classrooms, and the bathroom helped keep him from disappearing, and to not get into other people's cubbies and backpacks.

- Adult supervision at ALL TIMES when using the computer. Encouraged password protection and restriction of inappropriate websites.

- Encouraged teachers to lock up cell phones, iPads, and other valuables. During his school years, he stole and hid many things. He would bring home small insignificant little plastic toys that weren't his or rocks off the playground. Sometimes he got away with more valuable items such as a cell phone or iPad. For him, it wasn't the value of what he'd taken; it was the adrenalin rush!

  Because he was well-liked by his teachers, it was hard for them to believe me when I listed his behaviors, including stealing, at the beginning of the year. Eventually, they understood after they were caught off-guard. I told them if something had disappeared, think of Tyler first. They would first carefully retrace steps, ask several students, and most often, would eventually narrow it down to him. Of course, he would always deny any involvement. Between the teachers and my probing, I could often get a "version" of the truth from him. His pat answer was that he found it on the playground. Then he would move it from one hiding place to another. Sometimes, the teachers found the item several days later and sometimes not.

Once I received an email from a teacher with an attached picture of basketball shoes, inquiring if they were his. He carried them around for a few days but never put them on his feet, which was a red flag for his teacher. Of course, they were not his shoes. I later found out that he would leave them on the seat of the bus so I wouldn't see them when he came home. After getting on the bus the next morning, he would retrieve the shoes and then carry them all day long. After his teacher found out they weren't his, she took them to find the actual owner. To this day, I still do not know to whom those shoes belonged!

- Set up an emergency communication system from the school in case your child needs some immediate correction. I encouraged the teacher to call me at any time if Tyler was uncooperative. I could then immediately speak to him by phone to reinforce what he needed to do *now* to correct his behavior and lay out his consequences for not doing so. One incentive that worked was my threatening to go to his classroom and sit there with him during the school day if his behavior didn't improve. I only had to show up one time to let him know I was serious. The day I showed up to sit in his classroom with him he was surprised and very unhappy. From then on, I only had to remind him I would do it again if necessary.

- Monitor homework, class assignments, behavioral plans, IEPs, and use your communication system with the teacher if you have concerns.

- Request case conferences at least once a semester that include his "village." There were a variety of attendees, including Tyler's current teachers, school psychologist, learning advocates, and perhaps his private psychologist or tutor. These conferences helped to keep everyone on the same page. It amazed me that each person who interacted with my son had a slightly different view of him and how they handled certain behaviors differently. The whole of the input from everyone at the conferences created a more unified effective plan of action.

- Create a "village" of advocates in the school and nurture a relationship with them. Support them with thank you gift cards, movie tickets, and lots of compliments. They, in turn, will also compliment you and give you positive feedback that is extremely helpful in your journey. It goes a long way when you tell someone they are doing a great job and in turn, when you get told you are also doing a great job - especially when you don't always feel that you are.

- He had to switch to a new school for seventh grade. This change meant another transition, fraught with anxiety on our part. We had to make new connections, and Tyler was expected to have more autonomy. One of the things that worked the best was having the transition case conference described in Chapter 5. We didn't realize then how valuable the Significant Special Needs (SSN) Program, implemented in middle school would become over the next seven years. The team reassured us that children like Tyler tend to gravitate towards peers with similar issues in middle and high school years.

Supplemental Learning Programs

During the summer, Mom and I researched different programs and strategies that are promoted to help improve learning. Brain Balance and Learning RX are designed to help improve cognitive functioning and have been promoted as useful for some children. These did not fit our needs for a variety of reasons – cost, location, mixed outcome results. We also explored EMDR (Eye Movement Desensitization and Reprocessing) therapy for anxiety and depression. It was not something we wanted to try since it involved psychotherapy, and Tyler didn't have insight. We received many ideas from well-meaning people. Several ideas suggested were nutrition modification eliminating "allergens," equine (horse-riding) therapy, and others, but we had our hands full and had limited time. The summer he was 17, he started equine therapy and loved it. I wish I had the time and energy to have started it earlier.

One technique we tried was EEG Neurofeedback with a psychologist. It is a non-invasive therapy, proven to be effective in some children and adults with ADHD. EEG Neurofeedback is promoted to be without risk of side effects and is used to re-train the brain to regulate brain arousal. Tyler showed some improvement in his brain patterns, but at the time, we learned he did not think globally. He could not take what he learned in one situation and transfer that knowledge to the next one. To be effective, he needed to have more sessions, but the psychologist's office was far away, limiting our ability to transport him as frequently as was needed for optimum results. If you want more information on this, see Dr. Gray's book (Gray, 2004) in the Bibliography.

We enrolled him at one of the private tutoring centers, but that didn't work because of the inconsistencies of the tutors' schedules and his challenging behaviors. Finally, we found a terrific private tutor, who was also a special-needs teacher. She understood how to handle Tyler and has been effective in helping him with homework and improving his reading and math skills. After seven years, she is still in our lives, tutoring him at least a couple of times a month. It has taken lots of trial and error, but we finally found something that worked.

Private Schools

Tyler's high-level behaviors and lower intellectual IQ limited our choices. Many schools are unequipped to deal with children with special needs, who need line-of-sight supervision. Other factors such as locations, high costs, and lack of transportation were problems for me. We did find a couple of schools that were outstanding, but were very expensive and too far away. One of the private schools we visited suggested that he would do best in public schools because of the federally-mandated programs that were available to him.

Dana deserves a lot of credit for her creativity and resourcefulness finding solutions to unforeseen barriers. The proverb "Necessity is the mother of invention (Plato)" certainly applies here. Tyler was complicated and raising him was a challenge. When she became a single parent, her life became harder. She was determined to provide a stable home life and rich experiences for him while continuing to work. Single parents have to go it alone much of the time. For her mental health, it was necessary to find resources for herself and him. Throughout Tyler's school years, she was always searching for ideas to help him learn and keep him out of trouble. These years have been packed with the tools that worked best for them. I hope that you will find some new ideas here that help make your journey easier.

Chapter 9
Beginning High School

Because of the fire incident at the end of middle school, I was fed up with all of Tyler's behaviors. Having no workable answers, I was at the "point of no return". I told him it was a "make it or break it" transition for him into high school. Fearing the worst, my mom and I spent many hours the summer before high school, making calls to group homes, crisis care placement, and respite opportunities in case he didn't transition well.

Fortunately, I think this transition may have been a turning point, and it went smoother than expected. He started to mature a bit, which seemed to help his behavior. Hallelujah! It was not "the cure", but it was a glimmer of hope. I thought he might be on the right path. These past ten years of keeping a tight rein on Tyler were starting to pay off. He was actually fun to be around when he was not acting out. As usual, all of the school staff, including his teachers, thought I was crazy for putting all the safety measures in place. However, those preventative measures were significant reasons the behaviors decreased.

Knowing his past, I felt strongly that at some point, he would try to steal or start fires again. One of his therapists thought that he could learn to cook simple foods in a microwave to avoid cooking with an open gas flame. She realized that he could still blow up a microwave just as quickly due to his curiosity about how things work. He continued to mature and has become adept at cooking in a microwave. At least I know he won't starve if he ever lives alone. The negative behaviors have also gradually decreased. I continue to gain hope for his future!

My husband and I were proud to see Tyler maturing, even though he was lagging behind his peers by several years. He enjoyed helping me prepare a meal. He learned how to chop, measure, and use the stovetop to cook. He was getting better at weighing vegetables at the grocery and selecting the best price for items, with lots of assistance. We were all trying to help Tyler improve his life skills necessary for independence. He could select his clothes, was fastidious at making his bed, and loved to clean. We enjoyed watching him evolve into a teenager. He still had an aversion to others and preferred isolation to interaction. With us, he was more even-tempered than he was with his mom. Dana got the brunt of his moodiness and temper tantrums, so it was a relief for her when he

had overnights at our house. Their routine included frequent counseling sessions and tutoring a couple of times a week. Life would level out for several weeks or months until the next crisis would present itself. There were lots of ups and downs during these unpredictable years with Tyler. But we were seeing slow improvement overall.

Chapter 10
Safety

Throughout the years since his adoption, Tyler has exhibited periodic unsafe behaviors. Thank goodness, since he's been with me, he has never tried to harm anyone. Part of this behavior is due to his extreme curiosity to investigate how things work. But he lacks the insight to see the dangers since he can't grasp the concept of cause and effect. There is also a motivating thrill factor (I call it the "heroin high" effect), which stimulates a release of chemicals in his brain creating a feeling of happiness.

One weekend soon after he came to live with us, my husband and I took him on an overnight trip to create some much needed diversion from our stressful lives. We had taken a drive in the mountains and were having an enjoyable day, or so I thought. We stopped at a convenience store to get ice cream and proceeded to the hotel. We were all in a good mood, and things seemed to be going well. Being happy and content, my guard was down. We snuggled with Tyler before bedtime and then proceeded to put him in his bed. Upon pulling back the covers, I noticed a pocket lighter in the middle of the sheets. I was speechless. I was so frantic that I didn't know what to do. I felt total betrayal by my son. After I called my mom for some much-needed advice, she calmed me down and then helped me through the process. Tyler admitted that he had stolen the lighter from the convenience store counter while his dad was paying for the ice cream. He had managed to hide it until he got into bed. Tyler said he wanted to see what it would do when it was lit. Thank goodness he couldn't figure out how to use it! I think the old proverb, "Curiosity killed the cat", might have come true this time. It sure did put a damper on that weekend and didn't help with my trust issue either.

Although I have mentioned some of these earlier, I thought it might be helpful to consolidate the safety precautions I've implemented over time:

- Use password protection for all accessible technology and the use of parental controls for television. Don't share passwords within the child's visual or hearing range.

- Use lockboxes for sharp objects, medications, and valuables.

- Use keypads for doors and chimes on important doors such as the bedroom and outside doors.

- Small motion-sensitive alert devices are available for windows or sliding glass doors.

- Sew pockets closed to discourage transporting items unseen.

- Use intermittent random "pat-downs" after coming home from school during the escalation of stealing episodes. I would check Tyler's clothing and shoes for items that he would take and transfer to "more secure" places later. He would store things in his sleeves, elastic waistband, underwear, shoes, and socks and then move them to hiding spots on the playground or home to his bedroom. These "pat-downs" have been a good deterrent for stealing.

- Use a clear backpack for use at school that you can order on the internet.

- We increased awareness concerning fires and electricity.

  o Cover electrical outlets; remove lightbulbs if they are a problem. My son would break them to study the insides of the bulb.

  o Lighters, matches, and candles – Avoid having them in the home or secure them in a lockbox.

  o Batteries – use toys without batteries unless under direct supervision.

  o Explore fire safety courses for children offered by the fire department.

  o Use line-of-sight at all times.

  o Don't leave pets alone with your child until, and if, they can be trusted.

- General home safety has been one of my biggest challenges. I have lived in a world of apprehension and dread that Tyler has been just minutes away from his next disaster. We have "Tyler-proofed" our house for safety to the best of our ability.

- The following is not a safety issue, but is a dynamic in our home, contributing to our environment. First of all, it's exhausting to be with someone all the time, even my child whom I love. Secondly, I work from home. During school holidays and summer vacation, I have to find alternative arrangements for him. Two parents can often relieve one another to cover their children's schedules. Because my husband worked out of the home so much, I was on my own a lot. After our divorce, this became a significant problem for me, juggling schedules.

- School Safety addressed in Chapter 8.

After we moved to Colorado, Tyler came over to our house for overnights. He had a chime on his bedroom door at our house too, to continue the safety precautions he had at home. We made a point of keeping the line-of-sight pattern that had been established, but we were slightly less restrictive than at his home. His bedroom in our house had a bedside

lamp and a few more things he could explore. His toys were in the same room where he slept, and I left my cosmetics, nail care, and other items in his bathroom. When he was in those rooms, he did have access to many things that he hadn't had before. One time, with the door shut, his curiosity got the best of him. When Tyler was unusually quiet, I opened his bedroom door, and he was trying to catch a leaf on fire by laying it on the electric light. He did an excellent job of getting it charred, but fortunately, it didn't ignite. I learned by trial and error what to remove and what he would leave alone.

Another time he took my nail clippers, and we never did find them. I realized that I needed to lock up anything I didn't want him to have in a lockbox or remove them. He loved anything that made bubbles such as dish soap, shampoo, and even a bar of soap. So guess who got to scrape the dishes after dinner? The sink was full of bubbles, and those dishes and Tyler were squeaky clean. When he took a shower, the shampoo and soap would disappear pretty quickly. Those were things that he usually didn't get to do at his own house, so it was fun for him to get to do them at Grandma and Grandpa's.

Another example of trusting our grandson too much was when I left him in the living room alone while I went into my bedroom. I peeked, and there was Tyler in the kitchen with his head tipped back, dribbling the chocolate syrup into it. None of these mishaps were serious, but I was never quite sure what he was going to think up next!

Chapter 11

Navigating the Medical and Mental Health Systems

Medicaid has been invaluable to us as a payment source, but the hoops I have had to go through to get medications and services were challenging. It can become extremely frustrating and time-consuming. There is little choice of providers, and the waitlist for receiving services is long. Thank goodness I also have private insurance as primary. Unless the provider takes Medicaid as a secondary payer, I have to pay the uncovered portion or go without service until a Medicaid provider is available. Psychiatric services are even more difficult to access. Mental health in-patient beds are limited, and sometimes children have to be transferred to a different town to be admitted.

Here's a Review of the Tips and Lessons learned:

- Introduce new medications slowly and change them only when it's absolutely needed. It takes time for the user to get used to new medications and dosage changes.

- Get the "right cocktail" or mix, of medications. This often takes trials and time.

- Watch for psychiatric side effects, regardless of how innocent the medication seems to be, including over-the-counter medications. Read the medication enclosure in the package, or online, and watch for psychotic behaviors if your child starts on a new drug. Since the Zoloft incident, Tyler has had psychotic reactions to an antibiotic for acne and another when he had an interaction between his anti-psychotic medication and a muscle relaxant for pain after back surgery. I now make a mental note when his medications have been changed so that I am more aware of adverse effects.

- Trust your intuition. You know your child. Talk to the doctor about your concerns.

- Get the right counselor. Is your child making progress? Is the counselor listening to you and working with you?

- Get the right physician. Make a list of questions before your appointment. Make it concise and prioritize items by importance. Do the medical personnel listen to you and work with you? Are they available in an emergency?

- Be alert for possible new mental health or psychiatric symptoms after new medications and other triggers such as significant life changes. After the first time Tyler was admitted to a psychiatric unit, I knew at some point we would probably be there again.

Applied Behavior Analysis (ABA) Therapy

We have not tried ABA Therapy due to the long waitlists and limited providers. My understanding is that it involves teaching parents how to use positive reinforcement for good behavior over time, to replace negative behavior. A Board Certified Behavior Analyst meets with the parents and the child and develops an individualized plan of care. Parents learn new ways of dealing with their child's negative behaviors. You can talk with your pediatrician about whether this would work for your child. Many insurance plans, as well as Medicaid, will pay for this with a prescription.

More information is available on the Autism Speaks website: https://www.autismspeaks.org/tool-kit/atnair-p-parents-guide-applied-behavior-analysis

Chapter 12
Bonding

For such a short word, bonding can be a complicated long process. Each of us brings a different perspective of what bonding with another person feels like. Bonding may also be one-sided. In a relationship, one person can have strong, loving feelings that come from within, while the other person may feel little or no connection at all. When a baby is born, it first learns about the world by its interactions with its parent figure, usually the mother. It receives cues by sending out signals, such as crying, cooing, and eye contact. The baby gets positive reinforcement by being picked up and comforted when crying, being fed when hungry, and getting reciprocal smiles and coos from the parent. The newborn learns to trust this person. The first two to three years of life are critical toward developing positive attachments. If children do not receive a reciprocal response to their needs, they learn to mistrust the parent. As they get older, their mistrust turns to anger, and the parent who has abandoned them becomes their target for the anger.

Foster care children have often come from homes that have been disruptive and traumatic, with inadequate parenting and neglect. They can't trust their environment or parent figures to meet their most basic physical and emotional needs. Older children have usually been in many foster care homes and become even more mistrustful of connecting for fear of being rejected or harmed again. They become survivors and often develop negative behaviors such as manipulation, lying, and defiance. Adoptive parents have to earn their trust.

I had many preconceived notions about the adoption experience. We were older parents and novices. I thought that bonding would be automatic for all of us. Now, I realize that bonding is a slow process over time. We missed the critical first five years of our son's life when bonding between parent and child usually occurs. I always looked for clues of Tyler's bonding – calling me mom, allowing my hugs, or turning to me for safety when he was afraid. When he was older, I felt fulfilled when he would reciprocate teasing, share feelings, or listen to my ideas. We continue to strengthen our bond over time. Now we share subtle non-verbal cues between each other – a raise of an eyebrow, or a tiny smile. I know now that Tyler trusts me and will confide in me if I probe and question him. If you are struggling with this process, don't get discouraged if bonding with your child takes a long time – often many years. If parents maintain consistency that can be counted on, parental bonding will eventually happen.

Tyler always seemed comfortable when he was with me or my husband. Like Dana, we didn't have those first five years to develop a bond with him, no cuddles or tiny baby to rock to sleep. No "first times" that we all got to share, like rolling over, crawling, first steps, and baby teeth. Bonding goes deeper than just one generation; it is demonstrated and reinforced between generations. I feel robbed that I didn't get to experience Tyler's first years with Dana. However, we made up for it by sharing stories and building our lives around this new child. Because of his Autism, he never liked to be touched, only tolerated hugs, and definitely no cuddling. Because he had missed a lot of experiences that biological children have growing up, we got to introduce him to all sorts of new things to which he hadn't been exposed. We went on adventures every time he came to visit. He learned to skate, ride a bike and scooter, explore museums, and also helped us around the house. We dyed Easter eggs, decorated Christmas trees, and baked cookies. I went to his first day of school with Dana and stood in the background while his mother took his little hand and walked him to the new teacher. Dana and I both saw how he clung onto her, hid behind her legs, and relied on her to keep him safe while he stepped into the unknown of a new school year. He definitely wanted his

mom, not me, at that moment. There was no doubt of his bond with her then. He still enjoys coming to our house for an overnight, and he now has his own TV (with parental controls) that he can watch in his room. Tyler and I have agreed on "one-arm, side-hugs" that work for both of us. We are a family!

Chapter 13

Financial Resources

Finding financial resources is a challenge that never seems to go away. Our health care and mental health systems are extremely segmented. There isn't one point-of-contact person to guide us or one agency that has all of the answers. We are, in large part, on our own to initiate finding financial resources for our children. In addition to providing physical and emotional care for our child, we have to do the research. Research takes a great deal of time and energy that we don't have. When I inquire about a service or funding, often the first answer I receive is that we don't qualify. If I'm persistent and keep asking questions and calling different people, I often find someone who has answers. We've been able to piece together different pay sources and programs to create a comprehensive plan of care to meet Tyler's needs.

ADA

The Americans with Disabilities Act (ADA) of 1990 established the federal law that created rights for persons with physical and mental disabilities and prohibited discrimination of them. Disability regulations are implemented according to **Title I** (Employment), **Title II** (State and Local Government), and **Title III** (Public Accommodations and Commercial Facilities). The ADA https://www.ada.gov/2010_regs.htm provides information to understand what qualifications a disabled person must meet and what special accommodations are required for them. Eligibility varies by age, level, and type of disability. Many of the disabilities our children have automatically create eligibility under ADA. Title II regulations specify what your child is entitled to under the law. Know your rights!

Starting the Process

Organizations guided by ADA regulations administer a variety of programs and services. The names of agencies that implement the same standards vary from state-to-state. If your child is already in the state system, then your child's case manager should be able to help you discuss options for services and determine eligibility. The case manager can help direct you in applying for Medicaid if your child doesn't already have it. If you don't have a case manager or Medicaid, contact your Department of Health and Human Services to start the process. If your child is in school, you can ask the school counselor to help you get connected. Often more than one pay source may need to be used to cover various services. Don't give up! Search the web and ask other parents of children with special needs. Contact local non-profit organizations that serve children with similar needs and diagnoses as your child and ask them questions. Be persistent!

Title II Benefits under the ADA

In Colorado, there are 20 regional Community Centered Boards (CCB) that were created under the Colorado Department of Health Care Policy & Financing. These CCBs assist in accessing services for individuals with intellectual and developmental disabilities. Check the link below for a brief overview of CCB services in Colorado and contact information by county https://www.colorado.gov/pacific/hcpf/community-centered-boards (Community Centered Boards, 2019). If you live in another state, contact the agency that administers the Title II benefits in your state. Developmental Pathways is the CCB that serves my county and has provided valuable ongoing assistance to access funding and programs that help with Tyler's care. We have a case manager who coordinates our services, provides resources, and helps to find him funding sources. See their website dpcolo.org for more information on their services.

The three major program areas of Developmental Pathways are:

1) Early Intervention Program – This program serves families who have a child up to age three with a delay in his/her development or a qualifying diagnosis. If your child meets the eligibility criteria, a service coordinator may assist you in getting in-home and community-based care. Examples of care are occupational, physical, speech therapy, sign language, audiology services, plus developmental, social, and emotional intervention, depending on your child's needs.

2) Case Management Program – This program helps determine eligibility for Medicaid waivers or state-funded programs, develops a service plan, finds providers, and monitors effectiveness and your satisfaction as a family.

3) Community Outreach and Family Support Services – The Community Outreach Program helps clients to navigate resources through a weekly resource newsletter, trainings, and connecting with others receiving services. Family Support Services include helping access respite services, professional medical and dental services, transportation, and obtain assistive devices such as wheelchairs, hearing aids, braces, communication devices, and other supportive devices. There are support groups and many other services available to families of children and adults with disabilities.

Medicaid Benefits

The Center for Medicare and Medicaid Services (CMS) is a federal agency within the United States Department of Health and Human Services (HHS). It works with state governments to administer Medicaid and the Children's Health Insurance Program (CHIP). Medicaid is a public benefit program that serves low and middle-income families, as well as persons with disabilities who may be over the financial limits of regular Medicaid. Amounts of funding vary widely from state-to-state and by the type of disability. The Children's Health Insurance Program provides low-cost health coverage to children in families that earn too much money to qualify for Medicaid, but not enough to buy private insurance. Medicaid Home and

Community Based (HCBS) waivers are made available to serve people who wouldn't usually be eligible for Medicaid. They help keep persons in their homes rather than being institutionalized. Don't assume that you're not qualified for Medicaid or other pay sources. If you don't ask, you will pass up the opportunity to find out what's available to your family.

Social Security Income (SSI)

Excerpts from the Social Security Administration's publication (2019), Benefits for Children with Disabilities state that:

> Children under age 18 may qualify for SSI if they have a physical or mental condition that meets Social Security's definition for children's disabilities. Your family must also meet income eligibility limits. The amount of the SSI payment is different from state-to-state because some states add to the SSI payment. Your local Social Security office can tell you more about your state's total SSI payment (p.1) … The following are conditions that may qualify:

- Total blindness
- Total deafness
- Cerebral palsy
- Down syndrome
- Muscular dystrophy
- Severe intellectual disability (child age 4 or older)
- Symptomatic HIV infection
- Birth weight below 2 pounds, 10 ounces (p.4)

Children with Autism Spectrum Disorders (ASD) may be eligible for SSI disability benefits if your family's income and assets are within the SSI limits. Childhood Autism is listed under Section 112.10 Social Security Administration's (SSA) Impairment Listing Manual (2019). Qualifying for this benefit is based on strict criteria and generally describes severely affected children. You can make an appointment with someone at the Social Security Administration to discuss your child's eligibility. I would encourage you to use an autism advocacy organization with case managers to assist you with the process.

Wrap-around Agencies

Numerous national agencies are leaders in providing information and referral services, advocacy, residential and individual services, and other "wrap-around" (comprehensive) services. These programs coordinate care individualized to a specific client's diagnosis or their limitations. Some examples of great wrap-around organizations are The Arc, Autism Speaks, and Easter Seals. Many other local non-profit organizations also provide wrap-around services.

State Dept. of Intellectual and Developmental Disabilities (I/DD)

The names and types of services vary from state-to-state, so it's important to check with your state agency for services for which your child and family qualify. You can find your state's contact person's information on the National Association of

State Directors of Developmental Disabilities Services interactive map in the Bibliography (NASDDDS, 2019).

I'm grateful that I have had the time to help Dana research many of the financial options that are stated in this chapter. We found that attending workshops and seminars on various topics was extremely helpful, from the perspective of the information itself, finding experts we can contact later and to interact with other parents traveling the same journey. Most seminars geared towards families with children having special needs will provide child care while the parents attend. We have been on many "field trips" together visiting agencies, schools, camps, and meeting with Social Security, physicians, and Tyler's counselors. Having a second person along helps in remembering all of the information we each heard for discussion later. Often I am able to place calls or do online research, while she works, to expedite applications and narrow down options. I'm amazed how well Dana has pieced together various services and pay sources for Tyler by her diligent pursuit of the goal.

Chapter 14
The Future

I hoped by the book's end I could say Tyler was "cured" of all of the problems thrust upon him in the past. I hoped that he would be living a typical life as a high school teenager. Unfortunately, that hasn't occurred yet and most likely won't. Much of his negative behavior has improved throughout the years. He is maturing with age, and he can control some of his actions better. And when he slips up, his episodes have become more tolerable, which helps. He now has a basic understanding of cause and effect and is beginning to understand that his actions do indeed have consequences. Tyler has also learned how to communicate better over the years but still requires prompting to "use words" to communicate and convey his thoughts. Overall, he is much more fun to be around and is very well-liked by everyone. Due to his gift of understanding intricate patterns and diagrams, he can build anything from a picture or illustration, without needing to read directions. Tyler is now reading at a fourth-grade level and can do simple math with a calculator but has trouble with concepts of money and time. I'm currently encouraging him to take the initiative to make more independent decisions, such as choosing his hairstyle, food, music, and entertainment. He is developing his own identity. I'm proud that he's come so far!

He will probably always have some significant underlying deficits due to his lack of reasoning skills and his blurred understanding of the concepts of reality versus fantasy. The frequency and duration of his behavior flare-ups are fewer but are more significant when he does have them because he is stronger, more aggressive, and devious. Over time, these traits may present him with more problems in life than solutions. Some behaviors will continue to improve. Negative ones that may persist (temper outbursts, manipulation, lying, stealing, and fascination with fire) concern me most since they could be very damaging. What will life look like at the end of high school and into adulthood? He still has time to mature. Now that he's approaching age 18, there are new opportunities for us to explore as he moves into adulthood. Only time will tell.

Reflecting on my journey over the last 12 years, I realize that my life has had many highs and lows, many challenges, and has been filled with a roller-coaster of emotions. Even with all of the angst-filled times, I am glad I have had the experience, and have survived. I have learned to see the glass "half full" with more optimism, instead of feeling discouraged and hopeless. I have grown tremendously as an individual, although my path was much different than what I initially imagined. None of us knows where our life is heading until "life happens."

When I started this journey, I never understood what it meant to have a child with special needs and with so many problems. I would never have imagined the immense toll it would take on me, everyday life, my marriage, and relationships with friends and family. It took a long time to accept, not resent, the ongoing daily struggles. Some days demanded much more of an effort than I thought I could bear. As long as I was able to find respite and occasional reprieve, I could accept the struggles that life threw at me. Looking back, I know that I can feel proud that I have helped my child become a more independent person developing a mind of his own. Knowing that he has come so far gives me some satisfaction.

It has taken me a long time not to feel judged by others for the decisions I have had to make. I can now accept that my parenting methods may be different from other parents, but they have worked for Tyler, so far. I recently was in a workshop where everyone in the audience had children of varying ages with special needs. We felt an instant bond, recognizing similarities of our children's issues and the struggles we face. We identified with and appreciated each other's tales and experiences.

The best advice I can give you is to take it one step at a time. A wise person said to me, "You may have to take it a half-step at a time, sit down, get back up, and try it again. You may be able to take only another half-step and then sit down again. Or you may be able to move forward a couple of steps before sitting down again. There will be a constant challenge." This process is exhausting, but it gets a bit easier with time.

As I look back, I realize that I *have* survived. It is a good feeling. In spite of setbacks and discouragement, I have better tools now to help me recover quicker from problems. I hope that you have found additional ideas to help cope with the day-to-day challenges of caring for a child with special needs. It takes perseverance for us to feel generally optimistic; it does get better (and easier) over time. It may not be the life you or I imagined, but at least we can look back and say that it has made a difference to our children. Tyler's progress is what keeps me going and optimistic for the future. I wish you the best for your journey as well!

We have come to end of this book, but not the end of Tyler's story. It's only the beginning for him. At age 18 he legally becomes an adult. We have begun to prepare him and ourselves for the responsibilities ahead. There is a transition program offered through the high schools available to young adults with special needs. He will be able to enhance his life skills, learn to be more independent and self-advocate, and explore career opportunities. Dana and I will be exploring housing options for him and find funding sources. He is growing up before our eyes. He's taller than all of us and shaving. Where does the time go? Even without a compass to follow, we will have challenges. With all of the support his "village" will provide, he will have a better chance at having a quality life as an adult than at age 5, alone and lost. There is hope ahead!

Epilogue

Right after I finished writing the last chapter of this book, Tyler turned 18. A few months prior to that, I had started preparing him to become more independent. I had turned over the responsibility of choosing his own hairstyle and color, choosing and preparing some meals, and teaching him how to budget his allowance. Thinking about his future, my mom and I began planning for the next two years in anticipation of our goal for him to become more independent over time. We helped him to apply for Social Security disability benefits, drafted a Special Needs Trust (SNT), and opened a checking account for him.

As his 18th birthday approached, Tyler had become more assertive with his opinions and exhibited frustration with nearly everything I said. I tried to ignore most of this behavior, writing it off as a "typical teenager." But he was becoming more intolerant of his present situation and the restrictions while living in my home. Little did I know, Tyler was plotting another escape.

Two months after his birthday, he became incensed at my accusing him of something he denied doing. He couldn't, or didn't want, to let it go and was unwilling to de-escalate. Tyler screamed in rage for two hours. I heard him yelling "You should be dead!" I was very apprehensive about what he might do next. However, he finally went to sleep. The next day after school, he came home, did his chores, took a shower, packed his bag, and left home. He had no money or food, no phone or I.D., and just left. After calling the police which resulted in a full-fledged search and rescue effort, he was found seven hours later. He had broken into a restaurant, vandalized it and a car outside, stolen two iPads, and tried to start several fires. In just seven hours while on his own, he managed to do all of the bad behaviors I worried about – uncontrolled temper, stealing, lying, and fire starting. After he left my house, I found evidence of previous attempts to start fires in his playroom. He is now living with his father until we find suitable housing for him.

I still don't know how his life will turn out or the ending to this story. Was this an experiment in being emancipated that won't happen again? I believe it will repeat itself since he has no remorse and no insight about how it could have resulted in a horrible tragedy. I wonder how much I influenced his life by the attention and nurturing I gave him? Or, as many experts believe, is nature (genetics) the more significant influence on our personalities and traits? Many children with severe problems can overcome their early tendencies; some cannot. As parents of these children, we need to know that our efforts aren't in vain but also to be realistic about the possible outcomes. There is always hope!

Appendix

Example of a list I used at the beginning of the school year introductory conference:

POSITIVE TRAITS
1) Good heart/Kind to others
2) Loves to be a helper and loves to be "special"
3) Wants to please and do the right thing
4) Great smile-lights up a room when he does
5) Good sense of humor
6) Good manners
7) Photographic memory of things he *wants* to remember (names of people, types of cars, types of movies, rap artists, etc.)
8) Good with using his hands to put things together

CHALLENGES/LAGGING SKILLS/LEARNING ISSUES-
Very low academically
1) Needs one-on-one support to produce work
2) Gets distracted easily
3) Trouble with "connecting the dots"
4) Cognitive flexibility
5) Executive Functioning
6) Social interactions-Social thinking
7) Coping skills

8) Hard time focusing when the medication wears off

9) Have hired a tutor twice a week to help out with homework

10) Inability to grasp concepts of time, patterns, etc.

11) Does not grasp abstract ideas or concepts; everything is taken literally

BEHAVIORAL ISSUES

1) Lying and manipulation-Can't be trusted

2) Sneakiness-line-of-sight supervision at all times

3) Stealing

4) Self-harming (choking or rubbing arm until raw)

5) Wandering

6) Tends to destroy items/No remorse

7) Does not understand danger/dangerous situations/safety issues

TECHNIQUES THAT WORK

1) Works better on a structured system with routine and boundaries

2) Works better on a "Red, Yellow, Green" system of some sort-Thumbs Up, Thumbs Down, or Thumbs in-between

3) Visual aids and cues

MEDICATIONS

1) Adderall at noon for ADHD

Bibliography

Please note that the resources below are only a partial list of many good resources available, but are the main ones I have used. Omissions are not intentional. Even though a resource may focus on a specific diagnosis, please explore it, as there is often information that can be used for a variety of behaviors that our children exhibit.

Child Welfare Information Gateway. (2011). *Adoption assistance for children adopted from foster care.* Washington, DC: U.S. Department of Health and Human Services, Children's Bureau. Accessed October 27, 2019 https://www.childwelfare.gov/pubs/f-subsid/

_____, 2015. *Postadoption Depression.* Washington, DC: U.S. Department of Health and Human Services, Children's Bureau. Accessed October 27, 2019. https://www.childwelfare.gov/topics/adoption/adopt-parenting/depression/

Colorado Department of Health Care Policy & Financing. *Community Centered Boards. (2019)* State of Colorado. Accessed October 27, 2019. https://www.colorado.gov/pacific/hcpf/community-centered-boards

Social Security Administration. *Benefits for Children with Disabilities.* January, 2019. Publication No. 05-10026. ICN 455360. Accessed October 27, 2019. https://www.ssa.gov/pubs/EN-05-10026.pdf

_____, 2019. (SSA) *Impairment Listing Manual.* Accessed October 27, 2019. https://www.ssa.gov/disability/professionals/bluebook/ChildhoodListings.htm

U.S. Department of Education. *Individuals with Disabilities Education Act (IDEA). (2004) Washington, D.C. Accessed October 27, 2019.* https://sites.ed.gov/idea/statuteregulations/

Books

Forbes, Heather T. and B. Bryan Post. 2006. *Beyond Consequences, Logic, and Control: A Love-Based Approach to Helping Children with Severe Behaviors, Vol 1.* Orlando, FL: Beyond Consequences Institute.

Forbes, Heather T. 2008. *Beyond Consequences, Logic, and Control: A Love-Based Approach to Helping Children with Severe Behaviors, Vol 2.* Orlando, FL.: Beyond Consequences Institute.

Gray, Steven, PhD., A.B.Pd.N. 2004. *The Maltreated Child: Finding What Lurks Beneath.* Colorado Springs, CO: Living Water Press.

Thomas, Nancy. 2005. *When Love is Not Enough: A Guide to Parenting Children with Reactive Attachment Disorder – RAD*: Families by Design: ISBN: 0-9703525-4-9.

Organizations/ Websites

The Adoption Exchange Colorado: https://www.adoptex.org/ Also has chapters in Missouri, Nevada, and Utah. Connects waiting foster children to potential adopting families. Provides information and education pre and post-adoption. Also click on *The Adoption Journey*, then *Post-Adoption Services* by state. There you will find resources including local support groups, respite care information, and many other resources.

Autism Society of Colorado: www.autismcolorado.org Provides information & referral, networking, advocacy, and support for all ages of people living with autism in Colorado.

Autism Speaks: https://www.autismspeaks.org
This website is full of valuable information for parents of special needs children, regardless of their diagnosis. Look under the Help & Information tab, and then open Information by Topic. You can easily find and research topics that pertain to your child. Look at the "toolkits" that have been developed through grants and collaboration, including the Special Needs Financial Planning, Safety, School Community, Advocacy, and Challenging Behaviors kits.

The Arc: https://www.thearc.org/
A wrap-around national organization that provides advocacy, policy development, support and programs for individuals with intellectual and developmental disabilities and their families. The Arc interactive map to find state chapters is:
https://www.thearc.org/find-a-chapter

Colorado Coalition of Adoptive Families (COCAF):
http://www.cocaf.org/
Provides information to and advocates for families at all phases of the foster-adopt/adoption/kinship process.

Community Living Alternatives' Resource Directory:
https://www.clainc.org/resources/
A list of Denver area resources and web sites for clients with special needs.

Developmental Pathways: https://www.dpcolo.org/
One of the 20 Community Centered Boards (CCB) in Colorado and serves the county in which I live. All of the CCB's offer similar services. See more information in Ch. 13 – Financial Resources, Title II Benefits under the ADA.

Easter Seals: www.easterseals.com
A wrap-around organization offering a wide variety of programs and services for people with disabilities, children to seniors. It is also the largest provider of camping and recreation services for people with disabilities in the U.S.

Nancy Thomas Parenting: https://www.attachment.org/
Online resources that expand Nancy Thomas' concepts presented her book. Also offers seminars/webcasts, support groups, and other great resources for children with Reactive Attachment Disorder and other behavior problems.

National Association of State Directors of Developmental Disabilities Services' Interactive map to find a particular state's intellectual/developmental disabilities (I/DD) agency address and phone number: https://www.nasddds.org/state-agencies/

National Sports Center for the Disabled: http://nscd.org/
Provides sports clinics, activities, and camps for disabled children and adults.

Parent to Parent of Colorado (P2P):
https://www.abilityconnectioncolorado.org/p2p-co/
Connects families of children with disabilities or special
healthcare needs to each other and to the resources they need.

T.A.C.T. "Teaching the Autism Community Trades":
https://www.buildwithtact.org/
Denver-based organization that provides small-group classes
and workshops in the trades for children, teens, and young
adults with autism.

Learning Support

Sylvan Learning Center: https://www.sylvanlearning.com

Learning Rx: https://www.learningrx.com

Brain Balance Centers: https://www.brainbalancecenters.com

EMDR Therapy: https://www.emdr.org/page/emdr_therapy

Newsletters & e-magazines

Adoption Week online magazine: https://adoptionweek.com/

Adoptive Families Magazine:
https://www.adoptivefamilies.com/
Provides a variety of articles for adoptive families. Lists parent
support groups.

www.ingramcontent.com/pod-product-compliance
Lightning Source LLC
Chambersburg PA
CBHW061957040426
42447CB00010B/1796